Toronto Child Abuse Centre DISCARD

I'M A GREAT LITTLE KID:

A program for the primary prevention of child abuse

FACILITATOR'S GUIDE

Sue Hunter, Audrey Rastin & Pearl Rimer

TORONTO CHILD ABUSE CENTRE ©
890 Yonge Street, 11th Floor
Toronto, Ontario M4W 3P4
Tel: (416) 515-1100 Fax: (416) 515-1227
E-mail: info@tcac.on.ca   Website: www.tcac.on.ca
2002

Second Story Press

NATIONAL LIBRARY OF CANADA CATALOGUING IN PUBLICATION DATA

Hunter, Sue
I'm a great little kid : a program for the primary prevention of child abuse : facilitator's guide / Sue Hunter, Audrey Rastin, Pearl Rimer.

Guide to accompany titles in the series, I'm a great little kid series.

ISBN 1-896764-69-X

1. Child abuse--Prevention--Study and teaching (Elementary).
2. Self-esteem--Study and teaching (Elementary) 3. Communication--Study and teaching (Elementary)
4. Child abuse--Prevention.
I. Rimer, Pearl II. Rastin, Audrey III. Title. IV. Series: Grossman, Linda. I'm a great little kid series.

HV6626.5.H86 2002   372.3'7   C2002-904271-2

Design by P. Rutter

Printed and bound in Canada

Toronto Child Abuse Centre gratefully acknowledges the financial support of
the Ontario Trillium Foundation and TD Securities.

Second Story Press gratefully acknowledges the support of the Ontario Arts Council and the
Canada Council for the Arts for our publishing program. We acknowledge the financial support
of the Government of Canada through the Book Publishing Industry Development Program,
and the Government of Ontario through the Tax Credit Program.

ONTARIO ARTS COUNCIL
CONSEIL DES ARTS DE L'ONTARIO

Canada Council   Conseil des Arts
for the Arts   du Canada

Published by
SECOND STORY PRESS
720 Bathurst Street, Suite 301
Toronto, Ontario
M5S 2R4

www.secondstorypress.on.ca

TABLE OF CONTENTS

SECTION I – INFORMATION FOR FACILITATORS

SECTION II – ACTIVITIES

INTRODUCTION & ACKNOWLEDGEMENTS

Child abuse is recognized as a pervasive social problem and continues to be of serious concern despite ongoing prevention efforts. Many prevention programs focus on teaching children prevention skills that presume a child is confident and secure enough to say "no" to an adult. Given that children are socialized to follow adult instructions, this is at best a mixed message. These programs also assume that children can seek help from someone when an adult that they know and trust has been abusive. Expectations such as these are unrealistic for most children, especially those who are very young.

The dynamics of child abuse suggest that children who are targeted are often chosen for the very qualities that prevent them from saying "no" or telling someone about the abuse. Vulnerable children, with low self-esteem, poor communication skills and a lack of understanding about how and where to get help are at greater risk of abuse. The purpose of this program is to build and strengthen the skills and abilities that lessen children's vulnerability to abusive situations.

The *I'm A Great Little Kid* program consists of six storybooks and this *Facilitator's Guide.* The basic concepts covered are: **self-esteem, communication, making choices, respect, touch, and how and where to get help**. Each book addresses one of these areas. The guide is divided into two sections: *Section I: Information for Facilitators* provides background information on understanding and recognizing child abuse, coping with disclosure and the legal requirements of reporting abuse. *Section II: Activities* consists of a series of activities designed to reinforce the concepts and messages in each book. **These stories and activities are intended to be used with children from ages four to seven.**

We wish to acknowledge Linda Sky Grossman and Petra Bockus, the writer and illustrator of the books, without whom this project would not have been possible. Nadia Hall's expertise contributed greatly to the development of the activities. Karyn Kennedy and Nelson Hillier shared their knowledge and expertise. Many thanks to Carolyn Crum for reviewing the final draft of Section II. Sandra Scodellaro and Ann Williams provided valuable administrative support.

We thank the members of the Advisory Committee for their insight: Carolyn Amell, Lynn Blanche, Barry Gang, Bernadette Hood, Barbara Lampert, Elaine Levy, Ruth Miller, Barb Pimento, Janet Sullivan, Spyros Volanakis and Shanti Persad.

Margie Wolfe and the staff at Second Story Press have supported this project through thick and thin, and we are grateful for their commitment.

Every effort has been made to acknowledge the source of all information and activities. In the event of any questions arising as to the use of any material, we will be pleased to make the necessary corrections in future printings.

KEY POINTS TO REMEMBER

Indicators do not prove that a child has been abused. They are clues that alert a staff person that abuse may have occurred. A staff person must report his/her suspicions to a Children's Aid Society and document the information. The final diagnosis and/or assessment of the indicators is the role of a Children's Aid Society.

Everyone has a duty to report a child's need for protection. All individuals who perform professional/official duties with respect to children have the responsibility under the *Child and Family Services Act* to report their suspicions of child abuse to a Children's Aid Society.

The staff person is responsible for making observations, documenting and reporting his/her suspicions to a Children's Aid Society, <u>not</u> for proving if child abuse has occurred. It is the role of a Children's Aid Society to investigate allegations of abuse and decide on the action to be taken on behalf of a child.

It is not the role of staff or supervisory personnel to interview the child or the parent to prove child abuse or family violence. In situations where there is uncertainty as to whether or not the indicators support suspicions of child abuse and reporting requirements, consult with a Children's Aid Society.

It is the legal responsibility of the person who initially suspects the abuse to report directly to a Children's Aid Society. Any additional suspicions and information must be reported, even if previous reports with respect to the same child have been made. Reporting to or consulting with a Children's Aid Society should not result in sanction or reprimand in the workplace.

If child abuse is suspected, and it is not reported to a Children's Aid Society, the child(ren) may be at risk for further abuse. The agency/organization is put in the position of colluding with the family/alleged abuser in keeping the abuse a secret. Staff may be criminally and civilly liable.

SECTION I

INFORMATION FOR FACILITATORS

DEFINING CHILD ABUSE

Child abuse is categorized into four areas: **neglect, and physical, sexual and emotional abuse.** While these divisions are useful in understanding abuse, it is important to realize that many children may experience more than one form of abuse.

Neglect

* Neglect is the chronic inattention or omission on the part of the caregiver* to provide for the basic emotional and/or physical needs of the child, including:

> - food   - safe surroundings
> - clothing   - personal health care
> - housing   - medical and emotional care
> - supervision   - education

* Neglected children who do not receive adequate emotional, cognitive and physical stimulation, physical care and nutrition may experience irreversible lags in development.

Physical Abuse

* Physical abuse includes all acts by a caregiver that result in physical harm to a child.

* Physical abuse may result from inappropriate or excessive discipline and, in fact, the intent may not have been to hurt the child. *(The Canadian Incidence Study of Reported Child Abuse and Neglect* (Trocmé et al., 2001) revealed that 69% of substantiated physical abuse cases involved inappropriate punishment.)

* Injuries may be minor in nature (e.g., a bruise), or more serious injuries causing permanent damage or death (e.g., shaken baby syndrome).

* Although cultural factors play a role in caring for and/or disciplining children, injuring a child is unacceptable.

Sexual Abuse

* Sexual abuse occurs when a person uses his/her power over a child, and involves the child in any sexual act. The abuser may be more powerful because of his/her age, intellectual or physical development, authority over the child, and/or the child's dependency on him/her.

* "Touching" is not the only criteria in defining sexual abuse. It includes acts such as: fondling, genital stimulation, mutual masturbation, oral sex, using fingers, penis, or objects for vaginal/anal penetration, inappropriate sexual language or harassment, voyeurism, exhibitionism, as well as exposing a child to, or involving a child in, pornography or prostitution. The child, by virtue of age and position in life, is unable to give consent to any form of direct or indirect sexual contact.

* The offender may involve the child in the inappropriate sexual behaviour through: threats (e.g., "If you don't do this, I'll have to go to your sister."); bribes (e.g., "We'll go and buy you a nice present after."); lying (e.g., "This is how girls learn to be good mommies."); and force.

*The term "caregiver" refers to parents, teachers and any others responsible for children.

Emotional Abuse

A caregiver who has a pattern of using any of the following tactics in relating to or disciplining a child is, by definition, emotionally abusing a child.

- rejecting	- corrupting
- degrading	- exploiting
- isolating	- not responding emotionally
- terrorizing	- punishing a child's attempt to interact with the environment

Exposure To Family Violence

Family violence is the result of an imbalance of power, the aim of which is to frighten, intimidate and gain control. Family violence can take the form of physical, sexual, emotional or spiritual harm. It is common for abusers to repeat the cycle of violent behaviour, with increasing severity.

The terms "witnessing" or "exposure to" family violence refer to the multiple ways in which children are exposed to family violence: directly seeing and/or hearing the violence; being used as a pawn by the perpetrator; and/or experiencing the physical, emotional and psychological repercussions of violence (e.g., a family member who is physically injured, child protection and/or police intervention).

The Canadian Incidence Study of Reported Child Abuse and Neglect **found that in all categories of substantiated abuse (i.e., neglect and physical, sexual and emotional abuse), family members or other persons related to the child constituted 93% of alleged perpetrators (Trocmé et al., 2001).**

Abuse can occur at the hands of individual caregivers or on a larger scale. Child abuse can also occur in institutional settings if:

- children are not supervised adequately;

- harsh and/or harmful disciplinary measures are used to control children, such as corporal punishment, isolation, withholding food, or restraints; and

- the knowledge of any abusive behaviour toward children in the setting is not reported.

CULTURAL CONSIDERATIONS

Children come from a variety of ethno-cultural backgrounds, religions, social and economic situations, family structures and lifestyles. Staff must understand and respect their own beliefs and the beliefs and practices of others, while maintaining a clear understanding of what is defined as child abuse in Canadian society.

Some cultural practices, however, do include severe forms of corporal punishment such as beating a child with a belt or other object. This is not an accepted form of discipline in Canada and is considered child abuse. An extreme example of a cultural practice that is seen as child abuse is female genital mutilation. This practice, although promoted within the culture of origin, is in contravention of the *Criminal Code of Canada*, the standards of medical associations, human rights and child protection organizations.

In working with children, educators need to be aware of where cultural perspectives, beliefs and practices may influence the perception of causes and dynamics of child abuse, including:

- gender roles and roles in marriage

- responsibilities for raising children and role of the extended family

- expectations of children's development and methods of disciplining children

- degree of confidentiality regarding family matters, contributing to isolation*

- extent to which the family's culture would define its actions as abusive*

- beliefs regarding healing*

- societal tolerance of exposure to and use of violence

- methods of problem-solving and conflict resolution

- response to authority*

These factors may also influence whether or not an indicator of abuse goes undetected and/or unreported. Staff need to remember that it is not their job to determine whether a suspicion of child abuse falls within a cultural context – consultation with a Children's Aid Society is the best route.

DISCIPLINE VERSUS PUNISHMENT

Discipline is teaching and guidance that helps a child develop judgement, self-control, a sense of efficacy, self-sufficiency and socialized conduct. Discipline is sometimes confused with punishment, particularly by caregivers who use corporal punishment in their attempts to correct or change children's behaviour. The following chart compares discipline with punishment.

Discipline	Punishment
• respects the child and his/her abilities (i.e., whether the child is able to understand his/her behaviour and the implications of such)	• is a reaction to a child's behaviour with little or no regard for the abilities of the child (e.g., whether the child understands why s/he is being punished)
• has an educational goal that is appropriate to the child's misbehaviour and circumstances	• has the objective of inflicting pain; is excessive or cruel; and is a release for the caregiver or an expression of the caregiver's uncontrolled rage
• presents the adult as an authority figure	• relies on the power and dominance of the adult over a child who must obey
• uses a variety of positive techniques (e.g., stating expectations to a child and the consequences should the child not meet them)	• occurs only after some sort of "episode" and may be the only form of correction used
• helps the child to develop internal controls and choices about behaviour to prevent unacceptable behaviour in the future	• uses external controls to deal with a certain situation, which makes it difficult for the child to know how to behave appropriately in other circumstances
• builds positive relationships and recognizes an individual's worth	• causes the breakdown of relationships, and is usually a humiliating experience

HIGH-RISK CAREGIVER BEHAVIOURS

There are many caregiver behaviours and responses to children that, while not intended to harm children, may constitute maltreatment or lead to child abuse should they continue. Learning other ways to interact with children is important if any of the behaviours listed below are exhibited by a caregiver.

* resenting the needs of the children in care

* always wanting to be in control of children and how children's behaviour is managed

* creating rules, limits and routines to meet the needs of the caregiver rather than the children's needs

* using or threatening to use physical force with children, including pushing, shoving and spanking

* humiliating children (by public embarrassment, criticism, insults and put downs)

* not understanding why children misbehave and not knowing or using positive strategies of guiding children's behaviour

* not knowing how to respond to difficult behaviours

* unrealistic expectations of oneself and/or the children

* feeling and showing a dislike toward a certain child

* having a hard time controlling anger or angry feelings

* feeling stressed out, tired and having difficulty coping; not willing or able to ask for help

* having a special relationship with a certain child by letting him/her do or have more, wanting to spend more time alone with that one child, or trying to keep the relationship with the child a secret

* not intervening to protect a child who is being physically or emotionally hurt or mistreated

* using excessive force when trying to protect oneself or others from a child who is "out of control"

* ignoring the laws that protect children and the child protection system

(Adapted from Dawson, 1995)

CHILDREN WITH SPECIAL NEEDS

Although we are still learning about the complex interactions between family violence and disabilities, two facts are well documented:

• children with disabilities are more likely to be abused than other children (Sobsey & Varnhagen, 1988; and Sobsey, 1995); and

• many childhood disabilities result from child abuse (e.g., traumatic brain injury as a result of shaking an infant, violence during pregnancy).

A number of factors contribute to the increased risks experienced by children with special needs.

1. Many people think that children with special needs do not experience violence or abuse. Some people think that individuals with disabilities are not sexual, or sexually attractive, or that no one would ever want to hurt them. In fact, it is the child's vulnerability, not "sexual attractiveness," that draws the abuser who is looking for control.

2. Children with special needs may have multiple caregivers, and are much more likely to live outside their natural families than other children. Children with disabilities who are placed in these settings are at an increased risk for child abuse as a result of their exposure to a greater number of caregivers.

3. Children with disabilities have unequal power in relationships. Children whose mobility is impaired are unable to escape. Children with disabilities may not have had the learning opportunities and social interactions with peers available to other children. This may leave them at a disadvantage because of lack of knowledge of appropriate or inappropriate behaviour. Children may be unable to express themselves, to disclose or ask for help if communication is impaired.

4. Children with disabilities are more dependent on their caregivers, which may include extensive care necessary for washing, toileting and dressing, and may not recognize a situation as inappropriate or abusive. Additionally, these children may be unable to tell due to a communication difficulty, or may be afraid to tell for fear of: not being believed; being separated from their families; or losing needed services.

5. Forms of restraint are sometimes used with children who have special needs. Restraining a child who is deemed to be "out of control" may be considered necessary to protect the child or others in close contact with him/her. The risk of hurting a child increases when there is: a lack of consistent reasons for restraining a child; an unclear definition of "out of control"; and a caregiver who lacks training to safely restrain children. Restraint may also serve to escalate a situation and therefore increase the risk of injury.

6. Cultural attitudes and beliefs about children with special needs have been linked to child abuse and violence, such as the belief that their lives have less value, they are less than fully human, they are incapable of suffering or they suffer excessively.

POSSIBLE INDICATORS OF CHILD ABUSE & OF EXPOSURE TO FAMILY VIOLENCE

The signs, symptoms or clues that, when found on their own or in various combinations, may point to child abuse are called indicators. Indicators may:

- be apparent in the child's physical condition and/or manifested in the child's behaviour;

- be manifest in the behaviours and attitudes of adults who abuse children, and cause others to question their care of children (although most adults who have abused children are not mentally ill, a risk factor to take into account is adults who present with some personal dysfunction, such as mental illness, personality disorder or substance abuse);

- be non-specific and common in children and therefore it may be difficult to assess why they are present, for example, bedwetting nightmares, clinging or increased self-stimulation — these may be related to stress in the child's life, such as marital discord, family illness or death; and

- point to a history of abuse, such as the re-enactment of adult sexual behaviour or explicit sexual knowledge inappropriate to the child's age and stage of development.

Indicators do not prove that a child has been abused. They are clues that should alert a staff person that abuse may have occurred. It is not the job of staff to assess the physical or psychological state of a child or others involved. It is a staff person's responsibility to report any suspicions to a Children's Aid Society. The assessment and validation of allegations of child abuse is the role of a Children's Aid Society and/or police.

DOCUMENTING INDICATORS OF CHILD ABUSE

All observed indicators should be fully documented. This process helps to put the information in perspective, assists staff in reporting to a Children's Aid Society and provides a record in the investigation and court processes. When documenting any information, it is important to:

- record the information as soon as possible, including dates and times

- provide a description that is clear and concise

- be objective and nonjudgemental

- avoid interpretations of medical, physical or emotional conditions, and what you think is happening

- record any conversations between yourself and the child, or any others relevant to the situation

- record what the child or others said, *using their own words*, even if they are "slang" (especially terms for body parts or sexual behaviour)

- provide a full description of any injury, including size, colour, shape and placement on the body

- hand write your own documentation in your own words, using pen

- cross out and initial any mistakes and continue documenting — do <u>not</u> use white-out

- include the name and phone number of the individual you spoke with at a child protection agency and/or police service, and any advice/direction given

- make sure the entry is complete, then sign and date it

- document suspicions of abuse in a separate record

- start a new entry if, at a later date, there is new information or further suspicions of abuse

> **Your first recording of the facts is your documentation — do <u>not</u> make a rough copy and then write it over as a good copy. Do <u>not</u> go back and change any of your original notes.**

POSSIBLE INDICATORS OF NEGLECT

PHYSICAL INDICATORS IN CHILDREN	BEHAVIOURAL INDICATORS IN CHILDREN	BEHAVIOURS OBSERVED IN ADULTS WHO NEGLECT CHILDREN
<ul><li>an infant or young child may:<ul><li>not be growing as expected</li><li>be losing weight</li><li>look pale</li><li>not be eating well</li></ul></li><li>not dressed properly for the weather</li><li>dirty or unwashed</li><li>bad diaper rash or other skin problems</li><li>for a child of any age in diapers, a strong smell of urine</li><li>always hungry</li><li>lack of medical and/or dental care</li><li>signs of deprivation which improve with a more nurturing environment (e.g., hunger, diaper rash)</li></ul>	<ul><li>does not show skills as expected*</li><li>appears to have little energy</li><li>cries very little*</li><li>does not play with toys or notice people*</li><li>does not seem to care for anyone in particular*</li><li>may be very demanding of affection or attention from others</li><li>older children may steal food, drink alcohol or take drugs, break the law</li><li>takes care of a lot of their needs on their own</li><li>has a lot of adult responsibility at home</li><li>change or increase in problematic behaviours (e.g., anxiety, repetitive or obsessive-type behaviours)</li><li>discloses neglect (e.g., says there is no one at home)</li></ul>	<ul><li>does not provide for the child's basic needs</li><li>treats the child differently from other children in the family</li><li>does not use services offered or available</li><li>has a disorganized home life, with few regular routines (e.g., always brings the child very early, picks up the child late)</li><li>does not supervise the child properly (e.g., leaves the child alone, in a dangerous place, or with someone who cannot look after the child safely)</li><li>may indicate that the child is hard to care for, hard to feed, describes the child as demanding, expresses difficulty coping with the child and talks about being "very stressed"</li><li>may say that the child was or is unwanted</li><li>may ignore the child who is trying to be loving</li><li>has difficulty dealing with own problems and needs</li><li>is more concerned with own self than the child</li><li>is not very interested in the child (e.g., fails to keep child's appointments, appears apathetic toward child's daily events, unresponsive when approached with concerns)</li></ul>

*This behaviour may be typical for children with certain special needs.

POSSIBLE INDICATORS OF PHYSICAL ABUSE

PHYSICAL INDICATORS IN CHILDREN	BEHAVIOURAL INDICATORS IN CHILDREN	BEHAVIOURS OBSERVED IN ADULTS WHO ABUSE CHILDREN

• bruising/injuries in unusual or unexpected area(s) of the body
 	
• a lot of bruises on the body
 	
• bruises in the shape of an object (e.g., spoon, hand/fingerprints, belt)
 	
• burns:
  - from a cigarette
  - in a pattern that looks like an object (e.g., iron)
 	
• wears clothes to cover up injury, even in warm weather
 	
• patches of hair missing
 	
• signs of possible head injury:
  - swelling and pain
  - nausea or vomiting
  - feeling dizzy
  - bleeding from the scalp or nose
 	
• signs of possible injury to arms and legs:
  - pain
  - sensitive to touch
  - cannot move properly
  - limping
 	
• breathing causes pain
 	
• difficulty raising arms
 	
• human bite marks
 	
• cuts, scrapes inconsistent with normal play
 	
• signs of female genital mutilation (e.g., trouble going to the bathroom)
	• cannot remember how injuries happened*
	
	• the story of what happened does not match the injury
	
	• refuses, is unable or is afraid to talk about injuries
	
	• is afraid of adults or of a particular person
	
	• does not want to be touched*
	
	• may be very:
	  - aggressive*
	  - unhappy*
	  - withdrawn*
	  - obedient and wanting to please*
	  - uncooperative*
	
	• is afraid to go home
	
	• runs away*
	
	• is away a lot and when comes back there are signs of a healing injury
	
	• does not show skills as expected*
	
	• does not get along well with other children*
	
	• tries to hurt him/herself (e.g., cutting, hitting or biting him/herself)*
	
	• discloses abuse
		• does not tell the same story as the child about how the injury happened
		
		• may say that the child seems to have a lot of accidents
		
		• severely punishes the child
		
		• cannot control anger and frustration
		
		• expects too much from the child
		
		• talks about having problems dealing with the child
		
		• talks about the child as being bad, different or "the cause of my problems"
		
		• does not show love toward the child
		
		• does not go to the doctor right away to have injury checked
		
		• does not use services offered or available

*This behaviour may be typical for children with certain special needs.

POSSIBLE INDICATORS OF SEXUAL ABUSE

PHYSICAL INDICATORS IN CHILDREN	BEHAVIOURAL INDICATORS IN CHILDREN	BEHAVIOURS OBSERVED IN ADULTS WHO NEGLECT CHILDREN

• a lot of itching or pain in the throat, genital or anal area
 	
• a smell or discharge from the genital area
 	
• underwear that is bloody
 	
• pain when:
  - trying to go to the bathroom
  - sitting down
  - walking
  - swallowing
 	
• blood in urine or stool
 	
• injury to the breasts or genital area:
  - redness
  - bruising
  - cuts
  - swelling
 	
• pregnancy
	• copying the sexual behaviour of adults
	
	• knowing more about sex than expected
	
	• details of sex in the child's drawings/writing
	
	• sexual actions with self or other children/adults that are inappropriate or not previously observed
	
	• fears or refuses to go to a parent, relative, or friend for no clear reason
	
	• does not trust others
	
	• changes in personality that do not make sense (e.g., happy child becomes withdrawn)
	
	• goes back to behaving like a young child (e.g., bed-wetting, thumb-sucking)
	
	• problems or change in sleep pattern
	
	• very demanding of affection or attention, or clinging
	
	• refuses to be undressed* or when undressing shows fear
	
	• tries to hurt oneself (e.g., uses drugs or alcohol, eating disorders, suicide)
	
	• discloses abuse
		• may be very protective of the child
		
		• clings to the child for comfort
		
		• is often alone with the child
		
		• may be jealous of the child's relationships with others
		
		• does not like the child to be with friends unless a parent is present
		
		• talks about the child being "sexy"
		
		• touches the child in a sexual way
		
		• may use drugs or alcohol to feel freer to sexually abuse
		
		• allows or tries to get the child to participate in sexual behaviour

*This behaviour may be typical for children with certain special needs.

POSSIBLE INDICATORS OF EMOTIONAL ABUSE

PHYSICAL INDICATORS IN CHILDREN	BEHAVIOURAL INDICATORS IN CHILDREN	BEHAVIOURS OBSERVED IN ADULTS WHO ABUSE CHILDREN
• the child does not develop as expected* • often complains of nausea, headaches, stomachaches without any obvious reason • wets or dirties pants* • is not given food, clothing and care as good as the other children get • may have unusual appearance (e.g., strange haircuts, dress, decorations)	• is unhappy, stressed out, withdrawn,* aggressive* or angry for long periods of time • goes back to behaving like a young child (e.g., toileting problems, thumb-sucking, constant rocking) • tries too hard to be good and to get adults to approve • tries really hard to get attention • tries to hurt oneself (e.g., uses drugs or alcohol, suicide) • criticizes oneself a lot* • does not participate because of fear of failing* • may expect too much of him/herself so gets frustrated and fails* • is afraid of what the adult will do if s/he does something the adult does not like • runs away* • has a lot of adult responsibility • does not get along well with other children*	• often rejects, insults or criticizes the child, even in front of others • does not touch or speak to the child with love • talks about the child as being the cause for problems and things not going as wished • talks about or treats the child as being different from other children and family members • treats the child differently from other children in the family • compares the child to someone who is not liked • does not pay attention to the child and refuses to help the child • isolates the child, does not allow the child to see others both inside and outside the family (e.g., locks the child in a closet or room) • does not provide a good example for children on how to behave with others (e.g., swears all the time, hits others) • lets the child be involved in activities that break the law • uses the child to make money (e.g., child pornography) • lets the child see sex and violence on TV, videos and in magazines • terrorizes the child (e.g., threatens to hurt or kill the child or threatens someone or something that is special to the child) • forces the child to watch someone being hurt • asks the child to do more than s/he can do

*This behaviour may be typical for children with certain special needs.

POSSIBLE INDICATORS OF EXPOSURE TO FAMILY VIOLENCE

PHYSICAL INDICATORS IN CHILDREN	BEHAVIOURAL INDICATORS IN CHILDREN	BEHAVIOURS OBSERVED IN ADULTS
• the child does not develop as expected* • often complains of nausea, headaches, stomachaches without any obvious reason	• may be aggressive* and have temper tantrums* • may show withdrawn, depressed, and nervous behaviours (e.g., clinging, whining, a lot of crying*) • acts out what has been seen or heard between the parents/partners • tries too hard to be good and to get adults to approve • afraid of: - someone's anger - one's own anger (e.g., killing the abuser) - self or other loved ones being hurt or killed - being left alone and not cared for • problems sleeping (e.g., cannot fall asleep, afraid of the dark, does not want to go to bed, nightmares) • bed-wetting* • tries to hurt oneself (e.g., eating disorder, uses drugs or alcohol, suicide) • stays around the house to keep watch, or tries not to spend much time at home • problems with school* (e.g., trouble paying attention, poor marks, misses school a lot) • expects a lot of oneself and is afraid to fail and so works very hard and gets good marks in school • takes the job of protecting and helping other family members	• abuser has trouble controlling self • abuser has trouble talking and getting along with others • abuser uses threats and violence (e.g., threatens to hurt, kill or destroy someone or something that is special; cruel to animals) • the child is forced to watch a parent/partner being hurt • abuser is always watching what the partner is doing • abuser insults, blames, and criticizes partner in front of others • jealous of partner talking or being with others • abuser does not allow the child or family to talk with or see others • the abused person is not able to care properly for the children because of depression, trying to survive, or because the abuser does not give enough money • abuser holds the belief that s/he has the power and the abused person has to obey • uses drugs or alcohol • the abused person seems to be frightened • discloses family violence • discloses that the abuser assaulted or threw objects at someone holding a child

CONT'D.

POSSIBLE INDICATORS OF EXPOSURE TO FAMILY VIOLENCE CONT'D.

PHYSICAL INDICATORS IN CHILDREN	BEHAVIOURAL INDICATORS IN CHILDREN	BEHAVIOURS OBSERVED IN ADULTS
	• does not get along well with other children*	
	• runs away from home*	
	• is cruel to animals	
	• older children may steal, hurt others, join a gang or break the law	
	• child may act out sexually, become involved in prostitution	
	• discloses family violence	

*This behaviour may be typical for children with certain special needs.

(Adapted from Rimer & Prager, 1998)

CHILDREN'S SEXUAL BEHAVIOUR

Children's sexual behaviour must be considered along a continuum, like other areas of growth. Many behaviours are to be expected, are healthy and within the normal range for children. Some behaviours are problematic, and are certainly of concern. These are the "worrisome" behaviours, and should not be ignored or seen as child's play. These behaviours may require some degree of redirection or intervention. Other behaviours are problematic, and may be dangerous physically or psychologically to the child and others. Staff may require consultation regarding these behaviours, as these children may need professional help.

The behaviours in the first chart are mostly seen in toddlers and preschoolers, but may also be observed in older children. The second chart focuses on behaviours common in older children (adapted from Johnson, 1996). An asterisk* indicates the possibility that the behaviour described may be typical for children with certain special needs.

SEXUAL BEHAVIOUR IN TODDLERS & PRESCHOOLERS

TYPE OF BEHAVIOUR	OKAY	WORRISOME	GET HELP
CURIOSITY BEHAVIOURS	• asks age-appropriate questions about where babies come from, sexual characteristics • children learn to name body parts	• shows fear or anxiety around sexual topics	• asks almost endless questions on topics related to sex* • knows too much about sexuality for age and stage of development
SELF–EXPLORATION	• likes to be nude • has erections • explores own body with curiosity and pleasure • touches own genitals as a self-soothing behaviour (for example, when going to sleep, when feeling sick, tense or afraid) • toilet training highlights the child's awareness of genital area • puts objects in own genitals or rectum without discomfort	• self-stimulates* on furniture, toys and uses objects to self-stimulate • imitates sexual behaviour with dolls or toys • continues to self-stimulate in public after being told that this behaviour should take place in private* • puts something in genitals, rectum even when it feels uncomfortable	• self-stimulates publicly or privately to the exclusion of other activities* • self-stimulates on other people • causes harm to own genitals, rectum

SEXUAL BEHAVIOUR IN TODDLERS & PRESCHOOLERS CONT'D.

TYPE OF BEHAVIOUR	OKAY	WORRISOME	GET HELP
BEHAVIOUR WITH OTHERS	• explores the bodies of other children when playing • if people are naked, the child likes to look • wants to touch genitals to see what they feel like • may show his/her genitals or buttocks to others • may take off clothes in front of others • sees these behaviours as fun, silly; may be embarrassed	• continues to play games like "doctor" after limits set • confused about male and female differences, even after they have been explained* • continually wants to touch other people* • tries to engage in adult sexual behaviours • simulates sexual activity with clothes on	• forces, bullies other children to disrobe, engage in sexual behaviour • aggressive scenes between people are shown in dramatic play • demands to see the genitals of other children or adults • manipulates or forces other children into touching genitals, adult sexual behaviours, simulating sexual activity with clothes off, oral sex
BATHROOM, TOILETING AND SEXUAL FUNCTIONS	• interested in urination, defecation • is curious about and tries to see what people are doing in the bathroom • some preschoolers want privacy in the bathroom and when changing • uses inappropriate language or slang for toileting and sexual functions	• smears feces • purposefully urinates in inappropriate places • often caught watching others perform intimate bathroom functions • continues to use inappropriate language or slang after limits are set	• repeatedly smears feces • continues to urinate in inappropriate places • does not allow others privacy in the bathroom or bedroom • continually uses inappropriate language or slang without regard for limits set

SEXUAL BEHAVIOUR IN TODDLERS & PRESCHOOLERS CONT'D.

TYPE OF BEHAVIOUR	OKAY	WORRISOME	GET HELP
RELATIONSHIPS	• plays house with peers • will role play all aspects of male/female lives to learn, explore, rehearse • kisses and hugs people who are significant to them • may exchange information on sexual discoveries • may imitate sex in a rudimentary fashion	• focuses on sexual aspects of adult relationships • afraid of being kissed or hugged* • talks or acts in a sexualized manner with others • uses sexual language even after limits set • talks or engages in play about sex to the exclusion of other topics	• graphically imitates or reenacts adult sexual behavior • displays fear or anger about babies and giving birth • physical contact with others causes anxiety • talks in a sexualized manner with others, including unfamiliar adults • sexualizes all interactions with other children and adults
BEHAVIOUR WITH ANIMALS	• curious about how animals have babies	• touches genitals of animals	• sexual behaviour with animals

SEXUAL BEHAVIOUR IN SCHOOL-AGED CHILDREN

TYPE OF BEHAVIOUR	OKAY	WORRISOME	GET HELP
RELATIONSHIPS	• thinks opposite sex has "cooties" • chases children of the opposite sex • talks about sex with friends, talks about having a boyfriend/girlfriend • older children play games with peers related to sex and/or sexuality • likes telling and listening to dirty jokes	• refuses contact with a specific individual(s) • uses sexual terms to insult or intimidate others • romanticizes all relationships* • wants to play games related to sex and/or sexuality with much younger or older children • continues to tell dirty jokes after limits set • makes sexual sounds at inappropriate times*	• hurts and/or avoids certain types of people (e.g., the opposite sex, women, men, people with certain features such as facial hair) • habitually talks about sex and sexual acts,* and continues after limits are set • sexualizes all relationships • individual child or group of children forces others to play sexual games • continues to tell dirty jokes even after being reprimanded
NATURE OF SEXUAL AWARENESS	• includes genitals on drawings of people • looks at pictures of nude people • mocks opposite gender • demonstrates personal boundaries (e.g., wants privacy in the bathroom and when changing)	• includes genitals in drawings of one sex and not the other • genitals are a prominent feature in pictures, or out of proportion to the rest of the body • fascinated with pictures of nude people • wants to be the opposite gender • becomes very upset when personal boundaries are violated*	• drawings may include adult sexual activity, sexual abuse of a child • hates being own gender • hates own genitals • demands privacy in an aggressive or overly upset manner

RESPONDING EFFECTIVELY TO DISCLOSURE OF CHILD ABUSE

Purposeful disclosure occurs when a child makes the decision to tell. If a child tells you about abuse, you are probably a meaningful person in his/her life. Accidental disclosure occurs when a sensitive adult picks up on certain indicators manifested in the child's behaviour, play, questions or worries. A child's disclosure of abuse, whether purposeful or accidental, is very difficult. Shock, denial, anger, anxiety, pity and disgust are all common reactions to disclosure of child abuse. Experiencing a wide range of emotions is normal when faced with abusive behaviour toward children. These reactions must be acknowledged and addressed in order for staff to be objective and appropriate in responding to a disclosure, and effective in their contacts with the family, colleagues, a child protection agency and other authorities. (Source: Rimer & Prager, 1998, p. 75)

> It is the role of staff to listen to what the child is saying, and carefully observe the child's behaviour. It is not the role of staff to press for details, or prove that abuse has occurred, nor to carry out the investigation. Such attempts could contaminate an investigation and jeopardize the process. When there is a suspicion that a child is being or has been abused, staff are directed to report to a Children's Aid Society, and to ask for further direction.

IF A CHILD DISCLOSES:

Control Your Emotions

- Try to be relaxed and casual.
- Try not to display shock, disgust, or disapproval of the alleged abuser. Children may deeply love the alleged offender, even though they have been in an abusive situation.
- Do not assume that the abuse was a terrible experience (e.g., when a child has been sexually abused, where the adult has been attentive and gentle, the child may perceive the abuse as pleasurable. If one assumes the abuse was awful, it will only add to the child's guilt).
- Be aware and accepting of your own feelings. If you feel that you cannot control your emotional responses, talk to supervisory personnel and discuss the situation.

Offer Reassurance

Reassure children by letting them know that:

- they were very brave to tell;
- you are glad they are telling you about this;
- you are sorry that this has happened to them;
- they are not alone — this happens to other children too; and
- you will do everything you can to help.

Respect the Child's Comfort Level in Disclosing

- If a child is telling, listen.
- If a child is quiet, do not interrogate him/her.
- Do not undress a child or remove clothing to view injuries.
- Do not display the child's injuries to others indiscriminately.

RESPONDING EFFECTIVELY TO DISCLOSURE OF CHILD ABUSE CONT'D.

Be Aware of the Child's Developmental Level and Use of Language

- Use language appropriate to the developmental capacity of the child.
- Accept a child's terminology or "slang" words to describe an event — this is not the time to correct the words the child uses or his/her definition or description of what happened. *It is critical for the investigation that the child use his/her language in giving the account of the abuse.*
- Do not interrupt or fill in any silences with your own words.
- Answer the child's questions as simply and honestly as possible.
- Refrain from using trigger words or adult terminology (e.g., rape, incest, child abuse, wife assault or jail), since they may alarm the child or hamper the investigation.

Ask Questions That Are Open-Ended, That Are Not Leading or Suggestive of a Specific Answer

- "Can you tell me what happened?" "What happened next?" "How did you get that bruise?"

Be sure to:

- ask only those questions necessary to confirm your suspicions, such as, "How did you get that mark on your back?" or "Where did you learn to play that game?";
- ask questions calmly, and do not suggest to the child what happened or who did it;
- refrain from questioning the child's account (for example, by asking, "Are you sure it was Uncle Ted?");
- refrain from asking "Why?" Many children do not understand the motivation and may understand a "why" question to imply blame; and
- resist trying to change the mind of a child who has recanted — coaching a child or suggesting that something did/did not happen will hamper the progress of the case.

Tell the Child What Will Happen Next

- Do not make promises you cannot keep. For example, do not agree to keep the disclosure a "secret" even if the child asks or begs you not to tell anyone. You may want to remain silent out of respect for the child's wishes, loyalty or the confidentiality of the relationship, but it is important to explain to the child that some secrets must be shared in order to get help or to keep people from being hurt. Reassure the child that you will share information only with other people who will try to help. Failing to report places you in collusion with the abuser:

  - without outside intervention, the abuse will probably continue;
  - other children may be at risk of abuse; and
  - if calling a Children's Aid Society is used as a threat, then the Children's Aid Society is seen as punitive and not as a resource to families in need.

- Do not answer questions for which you do not have the answers. For example, if a child asks, "Will Daddy have to go to jail now?" you can only reply, "I don't know. Other people decide that."

- Until after you have spoken to the authorities, do not promise to stay with the child.

- Do not tell the child to keep any of your discussions with him/her secret.

Reporting Suspicions of Child Abuse & the System's Response

THE CHILD AND FAMILY SERVICES ACT (C.F.S.A.)

In Ontario, a child is defined as a person under the age of 16 (i.e., up to and including 15 years of age). (C.F.S.A. 37(1))

DUTY TO REPORT

1. **<u>Every</u> person in Ontario, including a person who performs professional or official duties with respect to children** is required under the *Child and Family Services Act* to report his/her suspicion that a child is in need of protection (e.g., neglected or physically, sexually or emotionally abused or likely to be abused). The suspicion and the information upon which that suspicion is based, must be reported to a Children's Aid Society <u>immediately</u>.

2. The individual who suspects that a child may have been abused or is at risk for abuse **must report to a Children's Aid Society, and <u>cannot</u> rely on anyone else to report on his/her behalf.**

3. Any additional suspicions and information **must be reported, even if previous reports with respect to the same child have already been made** to a Children's Aid Society.

PROTECTION FROM LIABILITY

All persons making a report of suspected child abuse to a Children's Aid Society are protected against civil action, unless that person is proven to have acted "…maliciously or without reasonable grounds for the belief or suspicion…"

FAILURE TO REPORT

If a person who has professional or official duties in their work with children does not report a suspicion of child abuse, then s/he can be charged and fined up to $1,000. This emphasizes that a child's safety must take precedence over all other concerns.

CONFIDENTIALITY

The professional's duty to report suspicions of child abuse overrides any other provision that would otherwise prohibit disclosure by a professional or official. No matter what the relationship between people, one must always follow through on the duty to report suspicions of child abuse. (The only exception to this is solicitor/client privilege.)

MAKING A REPORT OF SUSPECTED CHILD ABUSE

- The person who suspects child abuse must report "forthwith" (i.e., immediately) to a Children's Aid Society. Inform supervisory personnel of your intention to immediately call a child protection agency. It is best <u>not</u> to speak with anyone else about the details of your suspicion until you have spoken with a Children's Aid worker.

- If unsure of whether or not to report suspicions of child abuse, consult with a Children's Aid Society to discuss the situation with a worker and ask for guidance. <u>No one else is in a legal position to decide if a report should be made.</u>

- In Ontario, the report can be made to a Catholic Children's Aid Society, Jewish Family and Child Service, Children's Aid Society, or, in some areas, Native Child and Family Services.

- Information on how to reach the nearest Children's Aid Society can be found in: the emergency numbers page at the front of the white-page telephone book; the alphabetical (business) listing of the white-page telephone book; or by calling the local police department.

- When making a report, stay calm and provide as much information as possible. **<u>Do not conduct an investigation to search out any additional details.</u>**

- If this is your first time calling a Children's Aid Society, tell the worker that you are unfamiliar with the process.

- Calls can be made to a Children's Aid Society any time of the day or night. During regular business hours, an intake secretary or intake worker will likely take the call, record the information and direct the case to a child protection worker. Calls made after regular business hours will likely require you to leave a message and return telephone number with an answering service. Indicate if the matter is urgent. An after-hours protection worker should call back soon after.

- In most situations, leaving a message is not sufficient — it is necessary to speak with an intake secretary or worker to make a report.

- If you feel that the child is in immediate danger, contact police.

- Although calls can be made anonymously, it makes it more difficult for authorities to follow up on the case, gather information and protect the child. Therefore, it is recommended that the caller leave identifying information.

- Do <u>not</u> tell a parent/caregiver about the suspicions or the report until after consulting with a Children's Aid worker. Speaking to a parent/caregiver before receiving permission from a Children's Aid worker could jeopardize the child and/or the investigation. Consultation is particularly important when: sexual abuse is suspected; the alleged abuser is a member of the child's immediate family; the child requires medical attention for injuries suspected to have been caused by abuse; there is a chance that the family will respond by immediately withdrawing the child or not being available for further investigation; and/or there is a chance the child will be further abused.

COMMUNITY RESOURCES & SUPPORTS

The following resources are provided for general information related to child abuse and family violence. To report and/or obtain consultation and information on specific cases, call the local office of a Children's Aid Society.

Canadian Institute of Child Health
885 Meadowlands Drive East, Suite 512
Ottawa, Ontario K2C 3N2
Tel: (613) 224-4144 / Fax: (613) 224-4145
www.cich.ca
e-mail: cich@cich.ca

Canadian Resource Centre on Children
and Youth
180 Argyle Avenue, Suite 316
Ottawa, Ontario K2P 1B7
Tel: (613) 788-5102 / Fax: (613) 788-5075
http://www.cwlc.ca
e-mail: crccy@cwlc.ca

Education Wife Assault
427 Bloor Street West, Box 7
Toronto, Ontario M5S 1X7
Tel: (416) 968-3422 / Fax: (416) 968-2026
www.womanabuseprevention.com
e-mail: info@womanabuseprevention.com

Justice for Children and Youth
720 Spadina Avenue, Suite 405
Toronto, Ontario M5S 2T9
Tel: (416) 920-1633 / Fax: (416) 920-5855
www.jfcy.org
e-mail: admin@jfcy.org

Kids Help Phone
439 University Avenue, Suite 300
Toronto, Ontario M5G 1Y8
Tel: (416) 586-0100 / Fax: (416) 586-0651
Toll Free: 1-800-668-6868
http://kidshelp.sympatico.ca
e-mail: karyn.mcmahon@kidshelp.sympatico.ca

Parent Help Line
439 University Avenue, Suite 300
Toronto, Ontario M5G 1Y8
Tel: (416) 586-0100 / Fax: (416) 586-0651
Toll Free: 1-888-603-9100
http://parentsinfo.sympatico.ca
e-mail: karyn.mcmahon@kidshelp.sympatico.ca

The National Clearinghouse on Family Violence
(NCFV)
Family Violence Prevention Division
Health Canada
Main Floor, Finance Building
10 Tunney's Pasture
Ottawa, Ontario K1A 1B5
Tel: (613) 957-2938 / Fax: (613) 957-4247
Toll Free: 1-800-267-1291
www.hc-sc.gc.ca/nc-cn
e-mail: info@hc-sc.qc.ca

Parentbooks
201 Harbord Street
Toronto, Ontario M5S 1H6
Tel: (416) 537-8334 / Fax: (416) 537-9499
Toll Free: 1-800-209-9182
www.parentsbookstore.com
e-mail: parentbk@attcanada.ca

Toronto Child Abuse Centre
890 Yonge Street, 11th Floor
Toronto, Ontario M4W 3P4
(416) 515-1100 / Fax: (416) 515-1227
www.tcac.on.ca
e-mail: info@tcac.on.ca

REFERENCES

Bala, N., Harvey, W. & Vogl, R. (1994). *Dilemmas of Disclosure*. Toronto: The Institute for the Prevention of Child Abuse.

Barker, Narviar, C. (1991). Practical Guidelines for Child Care Providers in Working with Abused Children. *Journal of Child and Youth Care* 6(3),1-18.

Chapman, S., Kozak, C. & Nesbitt, K. (1993). *A Guide to the Prevention and Detection of Child Abuse*. Saskatoon: Saskatchewan Child Care Association.

Dawson, R. (1995). *Preventing Abuse & Allegations of Abuse*. Toronto: The Institute for the Prevention of Child Abuse.

Finkelhor, D., et al. (1986). *A Sourcebook on Child Sexual Abuse*. California: Sage Publications.

Geffner, R., Jaffe, P. & Sudermann, M. (eds.). (2000). *Children Exposed to Domestic Violence: Current Issues in Research, Intervention, Prevention, and Policy Development*. New York: The Haworth Maltreatment & Trauma Press.

Gelles, R.J. & Loseke, D.R. (eds.). (1993). *Current Controversies on Family Violence*. California: Sage Publications.

Johnson, T. C. (1996). *Understanding Children's Sexual Behaviors, What's Natural and Healthy*. California: Toni Cavanagh Johnson.

Leach, Penelope. (1992). *Spanking – A Short-Cut to Nowhere*. Ontario: The Canadian Society for the Prevention of Cruelty to Children.

Osofsky, J.D. (1999). The impact of violence on children. *The Future of Children* 9, 33-49.

Renooy, Lorna. (1995). *You Deserve to Be Safe*. Ontario: DisAbled Women's Network (DAWN).

Rimer, P. (2001). *Children Exposed to Family Violence: Guidelines for Community Service Providers*. Toronto: Toronto Child Abuse Centre.

Rimer, P. (2002). *Making a Difference: The Child Care Community Response to Child Abuse, 3rd Edition*. Toronto: Toronto Child Abuse Centre.

Rimer, Pearl & Prager, Betsy. (1998). *Reaching Out: Working Together to Identify and Respond To Child Victims of Abuse*. Toronto: ITP Nelson.

Sobsey, D. (Summer 1995). Violence Against Children with Disabilities, An Overview. *Connection 4*. Toronto: The Institute for the Prevention of Child Abuse.

Sobsey, D. & Varnhagen, C. (1988). *Sexual Abuse and Exploitation of People with Disabilities, Final Report*. Ottawa: Department of National Health and Welfare (ERDS No. ED346620).

Sorensen, T. & Snow, B. (1991). How Children Tell: The Process of Disclosure in Child Sexual Abuse. *Child Welfare* LXX(1), 3-15.

Sudermann, M. & Jaffe, P. (1999). *A Handbook for Health and Social Service Providers and Educators on Children Exposed to Woman Abuse/Family Violence*. The Family Violence Prevention Unit, Health Canada. Ottawa: Minister of Public Works and Government Services Canada.

Trocmé, N., et al. (2001). *Canadian Incidence Study of Reported Child Abuse and Neglect: Final Report*. Ottawa, Ontario: Minister of Public Works and Government Services Canada.

SECTION II

ACTIVITIES

INTRODUCTION

Section II: Activities consists of a series of activities designed to reinforce the concepts introduced in the storybooks. Each component begins with learning outcomes, key words and a series of discussion questions. It is most effective to read the books with the children before doing the activities. To facilitate ongoing discussion, consider including the storybooks in the book centre so that they are readily available to the children.

Although the activities are divided into six components to correspond with the stories, there is overlap. For example, strengthening communication skills will also serve to boost self-esteem. It is suggested that the concepts be explored over time, recognizing that there is a developmental component to the abilities and skills that are being fostered and strengthened through this program.

These activities are intended to be used with children from ages four to seven. However, the best judge of the skills and abilities of the children in the group is the facilitator. The activities can be adapted to meet individual developmental needs. Most of the activities are designed to be done in small groups or as one of many possible choices offered during playtime.

The concepts can be further reinforced by extending the activities. When considering strategies to expand the activities, think about the cultural and language composition of the group of children. For example, there is an activity connected to self-esteem that involves gathering information about children's names (My Name Is For Me). Be sure that the baby name book that is used as a resource is comprehensive and includes names from a variety of languages and cultures. It must also be noted that the everyday routines and rhythms of quality early education provide opportunities to develop and reinforce these skills and abilities.

Before beginning the activities, review *Section 1: Information for Facilitators*.

SELF–ESTEEM

Storybook: *Now I see How Great I can be*

LEARNING OUTCOMES FOR CHILDREN

• Express individual thoughts and share experiences

• Listen to and comment positively on the contributions of others in group discussions

• Express thoughts and feelings about ideas in a story

• Recognize a variety of emotions and identify the sources for such feelings

• Communicate thoughts and feelings in reading and writing

• Expand vocabulary of words that describe emotions

• Share family values and experiences

• Enhance positive sense of self through feedback of others

• Demonstrate a positive attitude about other children and the ability to look for positive attributes in every person.

• Talk about special interests, abilities, likes and preferences

SELF-ESTEEM is a feeling of self-worth. It is how children "feel inside" about themselves. When children participate in activities that build on their strengths, it helps them to develop a sense of confidence and an appreciation of their abilities. Children who feel good about themselves are more likely to develop positive relationships and are less likely to be mistreated in their interactions with others.

SELF–ESTEEM CONT'D.

DISCUSSION QUESTIONS

Niron's self-esteem and confidence blossom when, after much effort, he overcomes a new challenge.

* What happens when Niron gets upset at school at the beginning of the story?

* When Niron gets frustrated, he breaks the buttons and hides his head. What else could Niron do if he is having trouble learning to sew?

* Niron learns how to sew a button and feels very proud of himself. What do you do that makes you feel proud?

* How can we help other people to feel good about themselves?

* All kids are special. Can you think of something special about yourself?

* It feels good to help others. In what ways can you help your friends?

* The teacher was very helpful to Niron with his problem. If you had a problem and needed some help, what could you do? Who could you talk to?

Key Words/Phrases

* Self-esteem
* Special
* Challenge
* Liking yourself
* Feeling good about yourself
* I am an individual
* Feeling proud (pride)
* Sharing

SELF-ESTEEM CONT'D.

ACTIVITY: I'M A "MAZE"ING

Self-esteem is increased when children feel competent and capable. The ability to accomplish developmentally appropriate tasks strengthens self-esteem. Sharing accomplishments contributes to children feeling proud of themselves. This activity also promotes the development of gross motor skills.

MATERIALS NEEDED

- a variety of materials that can be used to build a maze/obstacle course (e.g., big blocks, large cardboard boxes, chairs, tables, blankets)

INSTRUCTIONS

1. Make sure the children know about mazes and obstacle courses. Invite a number of children to work together to create a maze/obstacle course.

2. Ask the children to move the materials provided to a large, open space (e.g., gym, playground), and to build a maze/obstacle course.

3. When the maze/obstacle course is completed, have the children invite the rest of the group to take turns going through the structure.

DISCUSSION QUESTIONS

- How did you decide what your creation would look like?

- How did you feel when people enjoyed playing in your maze/obstacle course?

- How did you feel about yourself?

SELF-ESTEEM CONT'D.

ACTIVITY: MY NAME IS FOR ME

The recognition and honouring of a person's name is a source of self-esteem. This activity will enhance feelings of individuality and respect for oneself and others.

MATERIALS NEEDED

- pencil

- baby name book

- cards or paper, pre-printed with questions for each child's family:

  - Why was your child's first name(s) chosen? Is s/he named after someone?
  - Is there a meaning to your child's name?
  - Is there a family tradition or naming ceremony when a child is born?

INSTRUCTIONS

1. Give each child a card/paper to take home with the pre-printed questions for the family. Have the children ask a family member to help complete the questions.

2. Remind the children to bring back the card/paper with the information gained at home.

3. Have the children share the information with the group, so that the meaning and value of each child's name is heard.

DISCUSSION QUESTIONS

- How did the child obtain his/her name?

- Why is the name meaningful to the child or family?

- Point out commonalities among such names as Peter, Pedro, Piotr – they may sound the same, but they still maintain originality and individuality.

Note to Facilitator: For those children who may not know the origin of their name, use a baby name book to try to obtain the meaning. This will ensure every child feels special. For those children who are <u>not</u> happy with their name, be prepared to point out the positive association provided by the family or the name book.

Children's names are often associated with different cultural origins, places of birth and family traditions. This activity lends itself to an array of other activities that focus on the appreciation of other cultures, different places in the world, family trees, etc.

SELF—ESTEEM CONT'D.

ACTIVITY: TAKING CARE

Capitalize on young children's love of water play in order to emphasize the importance of taking care of yourself, personal safety and positive touch. This activity provides an opportunity not only for children to engage in sensory play, but also to develop nurturing skills.

MATERIALS NEEDED

- large water tub(s)
- multi-racial infant dolls
- hypoallergenic soap
- facecloths, towels
- diapers and clothing

INSTRUCTIONS

1. Set up the large water tub(s) for children to bathe the dolls, providing props to enrich the dramatic and sensory play.

2. Ask questions throughout the play to have the children focus on the topics of caring for yourself, safety and nurturing others. *This is also an opportunity to challenge and dispel any stereotypic beliefs about boys doing a "mommy's job."*

DISCUSSION QUESTIONS

- Why do you think it is important for the baby to have a bath?

- When you were a baby, who helped you in the bath?

- Now that you are older/bigger, what things can you do for yourself in the bath/shower (e.g., washing your hair, drying yourself)?

- What do we have to be careful about when washing a baby? when washing ourselves? (e.g., not getting soap in your eyes, not making the water too hot)

- What else do you do to take care of yourself?

Note to Facilitator: For older children, try and have a real baby come in for a visit. Focus the children's observations and subsequent discussion on how babies communicate their wishes, needs, and interests. Have them comment on what babies spend the most time doing, and how babies cannot take care of themselves at all. Talk about all the things children do on their own now that they are more capable. This activity can be further extended by making a list comparing the capabilities of a baby to those of a preschooler/school-aged child.

SELF-ESTEEM CONT'D.

ACTIVITY: HIDE & FIND

Children's self-esteem is strengthened by appreciating their own uniqueness, and feeling valued as individuals. This activity provides an opportunity for children to make a choice about something that is meaningful to them and share their feelings with others in the group.

MATERIALS NEEDED

• a note to parents asking that each child bring a personal item (not too valuable) from home that is meaningful to the child (e.g., book, picture, toy)

INSTRUCTIONS

1. Give the children the note to take home asking them to select and bring a personal item from home that is meaningful to them.

2. Before hiding the objects, the facilitator identifies them in some way (e.g., ties a coloured ribbon or puts a coloured sticker on each item).

3. The facilitator hides these objects in the room or around the playground.

4. Before the children are asked to find the objects, the facilitator has a brief discussion with them about respecting the choices and feelings of others to reduce the potential of children being teased about their choice of item.

5. When all the objects have been recovered, everyone is gathered together for a discussion.

6. One at a time, the children hold up the item they have found and everyone guesses to whom it belongs. The children have two guesses before the teacher intervenes and asks the owner to proudly claim the object. *It does not matter if they guess correctly. The emphasis should be on the reason why the "owner" felt it was important to her/him to share this object with others.*

DISCUSSION QUESTIONS

• Why do you think the owner of the object chose to bring this particular one?

• Can you describe how this object makes you (the owner) feel? What makes it special to you?

• Discuss the variety of objects that were shared, with the emphasis on the value and appreciation of differences and similarities.

Note to Facilitator: This activity can be extended to incorporate sorting and classification, learning about different countries/cultures, etc. depending on what children bring.

COMMUNICATION

Storybook: *It's No Joke, My Telephone Broke*

LEARNING OUTCOMES FOR CHILDREN

- Listen and respond to others in a variety of contexts (e.g., pay attention to the speaker; take turns speaking in a group)

- Use gestures, tone of voice, and other nonverbal means to communicate more effectively

- Identify feelings and emotions, and express them in appropriate ways

- Use appropriate vocabulary and oral language structures to express emotions in a variety of situations

- Learn the importance of listening carefully

- Demonstrate careful listening and interpretation skills

- Enhance empathy for others

- Enhance awareness of verbal and nonverbal communication

- Practice reasoning and problem-solving

- Enhance expressive and descriptive language skills

- Foster appreciation of individuality

COMMUNICATION is the process of sending and receiving verbal and nonverbal messages. It involves understanding feelings and recognizing that everyone has the right to express feelings without infringing on the rights of others. Children increase their skill and confidence as communicators when they receive the support they need to talk about what is important to them.

COMMUNICATION CONT'D.

DISCUSSION QUESTIONS

The much-loved game of Broken Telephone shows the importance of communicating — hearing and listening carefully.

- Listening carefully when others are speaking is very important. What happens when the children play the telephone game?

- Speaking clearly helps the other person to understand you. Were all the children in the story speaking clearly? How do you know?

- We can communicate with words, and also with our bodies. What kinds of things can we say with our bodies?

- Vesna was very brave to speak out, even though she was embarrassed. Why do you think it is important to talk about our feelings?

- It is hard when you try to tell someone something and they don't understand you. Can you tell us about a time when this happened to you?

- What can you do if this happens to you?

Key Words/Phrases

- Talking
- Listening
- Communication
- Understanding feelings
- Body language
- Speaking out

COMMUNICATION CONT'D.

ACTIVITY: BROKEN TELEPHONE

In the book, *It's No Joke, My Telephone Broke*, Vesna was reduced to tears because what she heard was not the initial message. This activity can be used to emphasize that good communication means careful listening and speaking clearly so that a person will be understood.

MATERIALS NEEDED

* none

INSTRUCTIONS

1. Before the game of Broken Telephone starts, review ways that children can speak and listen effectively:

   * speak clearly and slowly

   * pay attention when someone is talking to you

   * if someone is not paying attention to you, do not begin to talk until you are sure that you are being heard (*Ask the children "How do you know when someone is listening to you?"*)

2. Have the children sit in a circle. The facilitator quietly whispers in the ear of the first person one of the phrases suggested below, and then tells him/her to pass it on to the next person, until everyone has heard the same phrase. The last person is asked to repeat the phrase out loud.

   For younger children start with a 3-4 word phrase/sentence:

   * I hugged a bug.

   * We danced after dinner.

   * We swam in the sea.

   For older children increase the sentence to 6-7 words:

   * The cat is wearing a hat.

   * My father made a marshmallow bar.

   * Lucy loves to lick ice cream cones.

DISCUSSION QUESTIONS

* Did the phrase change? How?

* What can you do to help people understand what you are telling them?

* What can you do to show that you are listening?

COMMUNICATION CONT'D.

ACTIVITY: YARN TOSS

Children need practice to become effective communicators, particularly in situations that they perceive as negative or hurtful to their sense of self. This activity allows children to practice responding to positive and negative statements. This activity also provides the opportunity to discuss how personal statements make them feel.

MATERIALS NEEDED

- ball of yarn

INSTRUCTIONS

1. The facilitator introduces this activity by asking the children to remember a time when they worked on a task and their efforts were criticized and not appreciated. *How did this make them feel?*

2. Tell the group that they will now play a game where the facilitator will start to say something "kind" or "unkind."

3. The facilitator holds onto the end of the yarn, and then tosses the ball of yarn to a child.

4. When the child catches the ball of yarn, the facilitator asks him/her to listen carefully to the beginning of the next sentence, so the child can then complete the sentence (see examples below).

5. The child is then instructed to hold onto his/her piece of yarn with one hand, and tosses the rest of the ball of yarn with the other hand to another child.

6. Numbers 4 and 5 above are repeated until all the children have had a turn. The yarn unravels creating a web each time a child tosses the ball of yarn to someone else while holding onto her/his segment.

Examples:
- Leaving out a friend in a game is...
- Offering someone help with a project is...
- Pushing someone out of line to get a turn faster is...
- Helping someone who got hurt on the playground is...
- Calling someone a name is...
- Grabbing toys away from someone is...
- Sharing a snack with someone who forgot his/hers at home is...
- Telling someone that s/he had a stupid idea is...
- Bringing food from home for a class pet is...

COMMUNICATION CONT'D.

Note to Facilitator: If a child has difficulty in creating a response, the facilitator can invite the group to help out with positive suggestions. The statements should <u>not</u> be personalized.

DISCUSSION QUESTIONS

* Which statements were positive and which ones were negative? Why?

* Was it hard to finish a statement in a positive way? Why or why not?

COMMUNICATION CONT'D.

ACTIVITY: SILENT MESSAGES

It is important for children to become aware of the many different ways they can use their bodies to communicate without using spoken language. This activity assists them in recognizing the different signals that are made through sound, gestures and facial expressions that may communicate different messages (e.g., clapping when happy, yawning when bored or tired, stamping feet when angry or frustrated, etc.).

MATERIALS NEEDED

* none

INSTRUCTIONS

1. In a circle, begin the activity by asking the children to think how they can use their bodies to communicate how they feel or what they are thinking.

2. Encourage each child to take a turn making a sound, a gesture or a facial expression and have the others imitate. Such nonverbal actions might include:

• waving	• crying
• humming	• frowning
• smiling	• clapping hands
• laughing	• yawning
• licking lips	• closing eyes

3. Have the other children guess what each person is trying to communicate.

DISCUSSION QUESTIONS

* What message were you communicating when you waved? cried? etc.

* Did everyone understand the messages being sent? Why or why not?

* How did you feel when you understood what someone was trying to say without using words?

* How did you feel when you did not understand what someone was trying to say when s/he did not use words?

COMMUNICATION CONT'D.

ACTIVITY: LISTEN, WHO IS TALKING NOW?

Each child's voice is unique and special. Part of communication is the ability to listen to others. This activity gives children opportunities to practice their listening skills.

MATERIALS NEEDED

- tape recorder

- audio recording tape

INSTRUCTIONS

1. The facilitator goes around the room while the children are playing, asking permission from the children to tape their voices while they are playing.

2. For the children who agree, tape their voices.

3. At an appropriate time, gather the children together and play the tape, stopping frequently to allow the children to guess whose voice belongs to whom.

DISCUSSION QUESTIONS

- How were you able to recognize that that was X's voice?

- When you couldn't recognize a voice, why was it difficult? What would have helped you?

- What two voices sounded alike? What voices sounded very different? In what way?

- Whose voice was the easiest to guess? Whose voice was the hardest to guess? Why?

MAKING CHOICES

Storybook: *Charlene's Choice*

LEARNING OUTCOMES FOR CHILDREN

- Use a variety of simple strategies to solve social problems (e.g., seek assistance from the teacher; talk about possible solutions)

- Ask different questions to gain information and explore alternatives

- Demonstrate age-appropriate decision-making skills

- Begin to develop own opinions by considering ideas from various written materials

- Use appropriate vocabulary and oral language structures to express emotions and decisions in a variety of situations

- Exercise individual and group decision-making skills

- Practice critical thinking and create solutions

- Improve gross motor coordination

MAKING CHOICES: Decision-making is the ability to choose between different ways of doing something, while considering the risks and consequences of each option. For children to learn to make healthy choices they need the opportunity to practice age-appropriate decision-making. Children develop confidence in their ability to make decisions when they know they can ask for help and support if the choices are difficult or confusing.

MAKING CHOICES CONT'D.

DISCUSSION QUESTIONS

Charlene is faced with a difficult choice — should she do the right thing and risk making her friend mad, or should she pretend nothing is wrong?

* Sam's butterfly book was overdue at the library. He told Charlene that he might not give it back. What does Charlene do?

* Sam really likes the butterfly book and wants to keep it longer, but the book must be returned to the library. What else can Sam do?

* Sam chooses to return the book to the teacher's desk. How did Charlene help Sam to make the right choice?

* If you think your friend is making the wrong choice, what are some of the things you could do?

* Charlene has a problem and goes to talk to her teacher. Who would you tell if you wanted help with making a choice?

* Everyday we make choices. What choices are easy to make? What choices are harder?

Key Words/Phrases

* Choices
* Identify the problem
* Make choices
* Consequence
* Take action
* Responsibility
* Problem-solving

MAKING CHOICES CONT'D.

ACTIVITY: HOW CAN I GET THERE?

This activity promotes the development of gross motor skills, and is a vehicle to encourage children to make individual choices. It is intended to be fun and support divergent exploration of equipment and body movements.

MATERIALS NEEDED

* Hula Hoops

* balls

* scooter boards

* tricycles

* skipping ropes

* other available equipment

INSTRUCTIONS

1. Tell the children that they have to get to the other side of the gym (either by themselves or with a partner) by choosing an interesting way to move their bodies using: one part of their body; two parts of their body; or their entire body (e.g., rolling, jumping, crawling, bottom shuffling, hopping on one foot, doing a wheelbarrow with the help of another person, etc.).

2. A secondary activity is to ask the children to get across the room, this time choosing one of the pieces of equipment available. Each child picks one piece of equipment and thinks of a new way of moving across the floor.

DISCUSSION QUESTIONS

* How did you decide to use your body in that way?

* Why did you choose that piece of equipment?

* Did anything help you in making your decisions?

* Did you enjoy your choice? Why or why not?

* What was different between the two ways of getting across the room?

MAKING CHOICES CONT'D.

ACTIVITY: WHAT WOULD I DO?

Key situations in the books, *Now I see How Great I can be*, *Respect Is Correct* and *Sam Speaks Out* are acted out using puppets to encourage children to consider how they would act given similar circumstances. This is an activity for children to do in pairs.

MATERIALS NEEDED

* a variety of puppets reflecting diversity of gender, race, culture and physical appearance

* cards with the situations written out (see below)

INSTRUCTIONS

1. Divide the children into pairs.

2. Have the children select their puppets.

3. The facilitator reads through the situations on the cards with the children and gives them time to work out a short "play" based on how they would respond to the situation. *The facilitator can ask the children to recall the actions taken by the characters in the book, but encourage them to come up with their own decisions about how they would act.*

4. The children can present their solutions back to the larger group.

Situations:

* You are at the lunch table when all of a sudden your friend sitting next to you knocks over the pitcher of milk and shouts, "Oh no! Look at the big mess I made." Your friend seems upset.

* Your friend is very sad. When you ask him why, he tells you that his next-door neighbour tickled and wrestled him to the floor. You said, "That sounds like fun." He answered that he wanted the neighbour to stop because the way he was touching him felt yucky. The neighbour got angry and told him to keep their secret and not tell anyone.

* One of your friends comes up to you and asks, "Do you want to play tag on the playground with me?" You really don't feel like playing tag. How do you answer her without hurting her feelings?

Note to Facilitator: Older children can generate different situations and solutions. The facilitator may also compose additional situations to discuss, based on actual events that have happened with the children.

MAKING CHOICES CONT'D.

DISCUSSION QUESTIONS

- How did you decide to act the way you did?

- Do you think you made a good choice?

- Was it difficult to make a choice about how to act? Why or why not?

- Could you make the decision by yourself or did you talk it over with your partner? How did your partner help you?

- Who else could help you make decisions?

MAKING CHOICES CONT'D.

ACTIVITY: WHERE CAN CHILDREN MAKE CHOICES?

Helping children learn to make age and developmentally appropriate decisions is very important. This activity requires that the facilitator think carefully about the daily routines and activities, and where the children have the opportunity to make meaningful choices.

MATERIALS NEEDED

- flip-chart paper

- coloured markers

INSTRUCTIONS

1. Prompt the children to brainstorm all the areas in the room and activity times during the day (e.g., large-group time, snack time, helper jobs, activity time).

2. Ask them to list things that they would like to make decisions about during those times and in those areas. Talk to the children about why grown-ups sometimes make decisions on behalf of children, and the types of decisions that children can make based on their age.

The facilitator may wish to consider creating a planning sheet that gets the children involved in the daily planning of their tasks. Such a tool provides the children with the opportunity and responsibility to experience a variety of activities and promotes organization of their time. This approach allows them to make choices about the tasks and when they will complete them.

The planning sheet would include headings of usual activities within which the children could choose their own tasks (e.g., language work, block corner, water table, meal/snack preparation, etc.). Decide how many tasks within each category they typically complete. The children then check off the tasks they will do and draw a line through the checkmark once the task is completed. The planning sheet can go home weekly so that the children can share with their families what work they accomplished and what their choices were during the week.

DISCUSSION QUESTIONS

- What changes could be made in our group that allow for more choice?

- How can we include what you have chosen?

- Who helps you decide if what you are choosing is safe?

Note to Facilitator: Using the children's feedback from this activity, expand opportunities for children to make developmentally appropriate choices throughout the day. This may require some flexibility and change in how routines, activities and meal/snack times are carried out.

MAKING CHOICES CONT'D.

ACTIVITY: IT'S MY CHOICE

This activity provides an opportunity for children to visually represent the choices they would make about what to wear in different situations. They will also be able to talk about how they make personal choices. This activity encourages discussion about the importance of respecting people's choices and individuality.

MATERIALS NEEDED

- mural paper divided into sections — each section has a picture of a situation/weather/ sport (e.g., a party, beach, picnic; a rainy day, snowy day, sunny day; baseball, swimming, soccer, etc.)

- magazines

- scissors

- glue

- crayons/markers

INSTRUCTIONS

1. Ask the children to look through the magazines and cut out pictures that represent what they would choose to wear in each of the situations illustrated on the mural. Older children have the alternative to draw and label their choices.

2. Have the children glue their pictures on the mural where they choose.

DISCUSSION QUESTIONS

- How did you make your choice of what to wear?

- When you get up in the morning, how do you choose your clothes?

Note to Facilitator: Reinforce the message that a person can still be polite and respectful even if s/he does not understand someone's choice (e.g., that means not saying things like "Yuk, you would wear that?" or "That's stupid, wearing a raincoat in the snow.").

Whenever possible, provide children with developmentally appropriate opportunities to choose their own clothes (e.g., a sweater or jacket).

RESPECT

Storybook: *Respect Is Correct*

LEARNING OUTCOMES FOR CHILDREN

- Demonstrate consideration for others by helping them

- Distinguish the similarities and differences between themselves and others

- Participate in group discussions, demonstrating a sense of when to speak, when to listen, and how much to say

- Value uniqueness of self and others

- Promote awareness and respect for individual differences and diversity in culture

- Use of a variety of problem-solving strategies for social situations

- Practice positive behaviours in response to bullying

- Use their creativity in movement and dancing activities

- Enhance feelings of empathy

- Use pictures to represent ideas and preferences

RESPECTING OTHERS is about treating people the way we want to be treated. It means paying attention to feelings, ideas, bodies, property and the desire for privacy. We show respect through our actions, our words and our appreciation of individuality. Teaching children about their rights and the rights of others demonstrates the importance of respect. Everyone deserves to be treated with respect.

RESPECT CONT'D.

DISCUSSION QUESTIONS

Jennie has trouble understanding the meaning of respect when the other children always make fun of her. By helping an older woman, however, she learns that in order to get respect, you first have to give it to others.

- Jennie and Amon talk about being teased by other kids. How does it feel to be picked on?

- Bullies are bothering a woman and her dog. What do Jennie and Amon do?

- When Jennie and Amon help the woman, how do you think the woman feels?

- If you saw someone being teased in the playground, what could you do?

- What would you do if you were being teased?

- What does the word "respect" mean?

- What could someone do to show they respected you? What would you do to show you respected them?

Key Words/Phrases

- Respect
- Disrespect
- Respecting differences
- Rights
- Equality
- Bully
- Bullying

RESPECT CONT'D.

ACTIVITY: NEWS ABOUT YOU

Building respect within a group takes time and many different approaches. This activity shows children the diversity that exists in one group of individuals. The discussion with the children should emphasize the importance of being respectful of everyone's likes, dislikes and personal situations.

MATERIALS NEEDED

- pencils

- a bingo sheet of generic statements that reflect the composition of the group, with space for the name of each child to be inserted (see next page)

Note to Facilitator: For younger children, put a pictorial representation in place of the written statement (e.g., a picture of books).

INSTRUCTIONS

1. Tell the children that they are going to "interview" one another. They will ask each other questions on the sheet (e.g., "Do you love to eat spicy food?").

2. The children are instructed to fill in only one person's name in each box. This means the bingo card will be filled with 9 names.

3. Once the sheet is completed, the child shouts "Bingo."

DISCUSSION QUESTIONS

- What did you learn about one another?

- Were you surprised by anything you learned about the other children?

BINGO CARD

_____ loves to eat spicy food	_____ loves to play soccer	_____ has a brother or sister
_____ is taking dance lessons	_____ has a pet	_____ loves to listen to music
_____ loves to play on the computer	_____ loves to bake	_____ loves to read books

RESPECT cont'd.

ACTIVITY: FAVOURITE FAMILY RECIPES

Food is a natural way to explore similarities and differences among children and their families. It provides the opportunity to share favourite recipes from home, while supporting emergent reading and writing skills. Cooking activities reinforce developing science and math skills. This activity is also an opportunity for those working in the setting to share their recipes.

MATERIALS NEEDED

- letter to parents explaining the activity and requesting recipes that are simple to prepare
- standardized recipe cards that are sent home to be filled out
- pictorial representation of recipes for younger children
- bowls, utensils, ingredients and cooking equipment as necessary
- flip-chart paper
- coloured markers

INSTRUCTIONS

1. Introduce this topic with a small taste-testing quiz. Have available small portions of different breads, fruits and vegetables that are representative of the cultures in the group.

2. Set out the food. Encourage the children to name the different food items that they are tasting. *Point out that all families need to eat, but that they all have different preferences in food. Encourage respectful comments even when children make negative statements about how something tastes or smells.*

3. Give out recipe cards and ask the children to take them home, along with the letter to parents.

4. When the recipe cards are returned, devise a schedule of what will be prepared so that every child may be included. For the actual cooking activity, ensure that pre-readers can follow the sequence of steps required for preparation by recreating the recipe in pictorial form (e.g., counting the number of cups/teaspoons/tablespoons needed; stirring, mixing, baking).

5. Spread this activity out over a period of time so that each child feels respected and valued.

Note to Facilitator: Invite family members to come in to assist. For recipes that are more complicated, invite the family to send in a sample for the group and review the ingredients and preparation according to the recipe. Reinforce the concept of respecting differences of opinion, tastes, preferences, likes and dislikes.

DISCUSSION QUESTIONS

- What did you like about today's recipe?
- Was this a new taste experience for you?

RESPECT CONT'D.

ACTIVITY: DANCING FUN

Music and moving to different rhythms are important to a child's evolving sense of self. This activity provides the opportunity to listen to different musical styles and rhythms that reflect a diversity of cultures, ethnic backgrounds and personal preferences. This also supports respect for and understanding of other cultures.

MATERIALS NEEDED

• tape recorder

• tapes of different musical styles (e.g., polka [accordion], blues [guitar and harmonica], klezmer [violin], calypso [steel bands], aboriginal [drumming], East Indian [sitar], etc.)

INSTRUCTIONS

1. Play a sample of the music (e.g., calypso/polka music) and encourage the children to stamp or clap out the rhythms.

2. Ask the children to move their bodies in any way they wish, in time to the rhythms.

3. Once again, play two different pieces of music that have contrasting rhythms and tempo. Encourage the children to move their bodies in response to the music.

DISCUSSION QUESTIONS

• How did the different types of music make you feel?

• What mood or emotion did you feel with the polka? blues? drumming? calypso?

• How did you want to move your body?

• Which music had a strong beat? Did that help you move?

• What kind of music do you listen to at home? Do your parents/siblings like to listen to the same kind of music?

Note to Facilitator: These questions provide an opportunity to discuss how age, experience and culture influence the music we like to listen to.

RESPECT CONT'D.

ACTIVITY: STOP THE BULLYING

The incident in the book, *Respect Is Correct*, in which an elderly woman is taunted and bullied, sets an excellent context for exploring positive responses to bullying. Part of becoming good communicators is the ability to recognize when someone is being discriminated against or treated unfairly, and then taking a stand against such hurtful or discriminatory behaviours. This activity asks children to think about what it is like to be bullied and to create strategies to respond to the situation.

MATERIALS NEEDED

- fact sheet

- pencils or pens

INSTRUCTIONS

1. Divide the children into small groups of 4 or 5.

2. Distribute the "Stop the Bullying" sheet (see next page).

3. Ask the children to:

   - choose 3 words that describe how they feel when bullying happens

   - generate 3 actions to resolve the problem of being bullied and witnessing bullying

For younger children, this activity can be done by having the children draw pictures or in small group discussions.

DISCUSSION QUESTIONS

- Has anyone ever been bullied? What did that experience feel like?

- Did anyone come to help you? How did that make you feel?

- If we had to create rules to help when bullying happens in our group, what would they be?

Note to Facilitator: The discussion and follow-up should connect protective bullying strategies for children:

- walk away
- walk/play with a friend/group
- never join in with the bully
- don't fight back

- tell someone you trust
- stay near the supervising person
- invite the child being bullied to play with you

STOP THE BULLYING

1. Can you think of 3 words that describe how it feels when bullying happens to you or someone else?

    1.

    2.

    3.

2. Someone is bullying you. What could you do to help solve this problem?

    1.

    2.

    3.

3. You see someone being bullied. What could you do to help solve this problem?

    1.

    2.

    3.

TOUCH

Storybook: *Sam Speaks Out*

LEARNING OUTCOMES FOR CHILDREN

- Recognize suggestions or advances that threaten safety or well-being (e.g., inappropriate touching, invitations to accompany strangers)

- Describe exploitative behaviours (e.g., abusive behaviours, bullying, inappropriate touching) and the feelings associated with them

- Describe types of verbal and physical violence (e.g., name-calling, kicking, hitting)

- Improve the ability to name body parts and talk about their functions

- Promote familiarity and respect when discussing differences in skin colour, physical appearances and ability

- Provide an opportunity to discuss differences in personal preferences regarding touch

- Improve tactile discrimination by exploring differences in textures

- Expand descriptive vocabulary

- Provide opportunities for sensory pleasure

- Promote feelings of nurturance and empathy

POSITIVE TOUCH is an important part of human relationships. Touch may be confusing because it can give mixed messages. For example, parents tell children to kiss someone good night when they would not kiss that person themselves, or a child is spanked as punishment for hitting a sibling. Children need help identifying the differences between touch that feels good, touch that does not feel good and touch that makes them feel uncomfortable. Most importantly, children need a clear message that <u>all touching can be talked about</u>. Children who know they have a right to say "no" or to question how they have been touched gain valuable child abuse prevention skills.

> <u>Before</u> beginning the activities on touch, it is important that the facilitator review the information on Possible Indicators of Child Abuse & of Children Exposed to Family Violence, The Disclosure of Child Abuse and Reporting Suspicions of Child Abuse outlined in Section I.

TOUCH cont'd.

DISCUSSION QUESTIONS

Sam has a secret that is making him sad and confused. Finally, he tells his friend. He learns that he has not done anything wrong, and that not all secrets should be kept.

- Sam was given a time-out for teasing his dog, Mac, but Sam was also upset about something else. What was Sam upset about?

- Some touches make us feel good. What kind of touching do you like?

- Some touches make us feel uncomfortable, hurt or angry. Is there any kind of touching you don't like?

- Some touches make us feel uncomfortable or strange. What would you do if you felt this way about a touch?

- **Everyone feels differently about touching. Some people like to be tickled and some people don't. <u>All touching can be talked about.</u>**

- Who would you tell if someone touched you and you didn't like it? What would you do if someone told you to keep the touch a secret?

Note to Facilitator: The most important message is that all touching can be talked about, and even if children are told to keep touch a secret, encourage them to tell someone they trust.

Key Words/Phrases

- Touch
- Good touch
- Touch that doesn't feel good
- Uncomfortable touch
- All touching can be talked about
- Secret
- Surprise
- Tell someone

TOUCH CONT'D.

ACTIVITY: "MY BODY BELONGS TO ME"

This expands on the body-tracing art activity that is commonly done with children, acknowledging each child as a unique individual. It provides an opportunity to reinforce the principle that "your body belongs to you" and that each child has the right to decide how s/he is touched.

MATERIALS NEEDED

- mural paper
- crayons
- paints
- stickers with happy faces
- stickers with sad faces

INSTRUCTIONS

1. Cut the mural paper so that it is long enough for each child to have his/her entire body traced.

2. Pair children. Tell them that while one child lies as still as possible on the mural paper, the other child traces the outline of his/her body.

3. Once the outlines of the children's bodies are traced, invite them to colour/paint on their faces, hair and clothes.

4. Distribute the happy and sad face stickers and ask the children to put a happy face sticker where they like being touched, and a sad face sticker where they do not like to be touched. (Alternatively, if stickers are not available, ask the children to put a circle where they like being touched and an X where they do not like to be touched.)

DISCUSSION QUESTIONS

- What body parts do you like to have touched?

- Who decides how touching makes you feel?

- What do you do if someone touches your body in a way that you do not like (e.g., tickling, stroking your hair, pinching your cheek, touching your feet, etc.)?

Note to Facilitator: Some children may comment that it is OK for a doctor/nurse to touch them anywhere and in any way. Clarify that someone whom the child trusts should be in the room with him/her for all medical examinations.

TOUCH CONT'D.

ACTIVITY: ALL KINDS OF TOUCH

Touch is an important part of our lives. There are many different reasons that we touch objects, animals and other people. Children need the message that <u>all</u> touching can be talked about.

MATERIALS NEEDED

- A copy of *Charlene's Choice, Now I see How Great I can be, It's No Joke, My Telephone Broke, Respect Is Correct, Sam Speaks Out* and *A Tale Worth Telling.*

INSTRUCTIONS

1. Show the pictures listed below from the books.

2. As the children are looking at the different illustrations of touch, ask them to describe what that touch means to them. Then ask how such a touch would make them feel.

Charlene's Choice

- Children in the field touching insects and plants

- Sam touching a friend at snack time

- Charlene embracing Sam

Now I see How Great I can be

- Niron touching Teddy on his bed

- A friend touching Niron as he goes up the tree to fetch the kite

- Niron cuddling Teddy at night

It's No Joke, My Telephone Broke

- One child pushing another child away during the telephone game

- The teacher touching Vesna's back

Respect Is Correct

- Kids teasing Jennie and pulling her hair

- Jennie taking the woman by her arm to help her up

TOUCH CONT'D.

Sam Speaks Out

- Sam teasing his dog, Mac

- Sam's teacher patting his head after he fell

- Sam sitting with his mother

A Tale Worth Telling

- Brian grabbing David's arm in anger

- David and his father hugging

DISCUSSION QUESTIONS

- What kinds of touch show that you are a friend?

- What kinds of touch do you think are unfriendly?

- What should you do if someone is touching you in a way that you don't like?

- What does it mean to you if someone pats you on the back or gives you a hug?

Note to Facilitator: Discuss differences in preference about touching, including cultural beliefs and values. For example, some children like hugging, while others do not. Again, reinforce the message that all touching can be talked about.

TOUCH CONT'D.

ACTIVITY: TEXTURES, TEXTURES

This activity allows children to explore different textures, develop vocabulary for descriptive words and express preferences about what they like to touch and what they do not.

MATERIALS NEEDED

- An assortment of different textured materials that could include:

  - feathers

  - velvet

  - various grades of sandpaper

  - dish scrubber

  - velcro

  - fake fur

INSTRUCTIONS

1. Ask the children to touch their faces, hands, feet, arms, legs and tummies with the different textured objects.

2. Offer descriptive words to help the children express the different sensations they are experiencing.

DISCUSSION QUESTIONS

- What does the sandpaper feel like against your foot? The feather against your cheek?

- Which material feels the softest?

- Which material feels the scratchiest?

- Which material do you like the feel of the most? Why?

- Which material do you like to touch the least? Why?

- Which materials feel like opposites to touch?

TOUCH CONT'D.

ACTIVITY: TOUCHABLE ART

This activity is open-ended to allow children to explore textures in an unstructured and creative way. This is a safe way to play with textures, even for children who may feel somewhat uncomfortable.

MATERIALS NEEDED

- shiny finger-paint paper

- finger-paint of different colours

- sand

- yarn cut in small pieces

- tinsel

- sandpaper

- textured fabrics cut in small pieces (e.g., corduroy, velvet)

- glue/paste

INSTRUCTIONS

1. Set up stations with the materials for small groupings of children. This encourages the children to observe others at play, comment and have a conversation about what they are doing and how it feels.

2. Allow the children to explore the arts and craft materials in any way they wish.

DISCUSSION QUESTIONS

- What materials did you like to touch? Why?

- What materials did you not like to touch? Why?

How & Where To Get Help

Storybook: *A Tale Worth Telling*

LEARNING OUTCOMES FOR CHILDREN

- Identify people who help others in the community, and describe what they do

- Communicate needs to peers and adults

- Identify people who can provide personal safety assistance and explain how to access them

- Explain the importance of being able to say no to exploitative behaviours (e.g., improper touching), and describe how to seek help

- Practice using a problem-solving process to identify ways of obtaining support for personal safety in the school and community

- Ask questions about the immediate environment and offer personal opinions

- Communicate ideas and follow basic instructions and directions

- Demonstrate the difference between telling and tattling

- Reinforce the importance of getting help when needed

- Improve memory and visual discrimination skills

KNOWING HOW AND WHERE TO GET HELP involves recognizing and reaching out to people who can provide support and encouragement. A support system may include teachers, doctors, nurses, counsellors and police, as well as family, friends, relatives and neighbours. Knowing when and where to go for help is based on trusting your feelings. Your feelings tell you when to seek help for yourself, your family and your friends.

HOW & WHERE TO GET HELP cont'd.

DISCUSSION QUESTIONS

David, the new boy, seems quiet and unfriendly. The other children discover that an adult has made him feel badly about himself. He is worried that if he talks about it, no one will listen or believe him.

- What is David upset about?

- Who does David try to talk to first about his problem?

- How do you think David feels when his sister and Dad were too busy to listen to him? What else could David do to get help?

- Niron and Vesna are good friends and listen to David's problem. What do they tell David to do?

- Mr. Green is a good listener and is helpful to David. How does Mr. Green help David?

- Who would you tell if you had a problem?

- What would you do if you went to someone for help and they did not help you?

> **Key Words/Phrases**
> - Support
> - Trust
> - People who can help
> - Trust your feelings
> - Secrets
> - Keep telling
> - Helping a friend
> - Tattling
> - Telling

HOW & WHERE TO GET HELP CONT'D.

ACTIVITY: A MAP OF OUR NEIGHBOURHOOD

Taking a walk around the neighbourhood provides a good opportunity to create a map of what exists in the community in terms of supports and good, safe places to be.

MATERIALS NEEDED

- sketch pads or paper on clipboards
- coloured pencils
- markers
- rulers

INSTRUCTIONS

1. Before going out to explore the neighborhood, introduce the terms "community" and "neighborhood." Ask the children what they believe these words mean. *Guide their thinking toward the concept that "community" functions when people help one another with services and finding support for things they need. It also includes a big emphasis on keeping people safe. Elicit from the children what they believe are the most important buildings and places to go in their community (e.g., school, library, park, fire and police station, playground, hospital/community health clinic/doctor's office, stores, recreation centres, place of worship, etc.).*

2. Go for the walk around the neighbourhood.

3. Upon their return, assign the children to work in pairs and ask each pair to draw a different piece of the community.

4. Compile the pictures and have the children arrange them in sequence of what they saw on the walk.

5. Generate a summary of all the supports and services.

Note to Facilitator: As an alternative to drawing, have the children construct their neighbourhood using blocks, people and animal props, boxes and tubes.

DISCUSSION QUESTIONS

- What are the things in our neighbourhood that make it a special place to live?

- Where can we go to in our neighbourhood if we want to play safely?

- Where in our neighbourhood can we go if we need help?

Note to Facilitator: Young children should not play unsupervised even in areas they define as places to play safely (e.g., the playground).

HOW & WHERE TO GET HELP CONT'D.

ACTIVITY: TATTLING OR TELLING

This activity will help children understand the difference between tattling on someone (i.e., to get them in trouble) and telling an adult about something (i.e., in order to get help.) When children learn that they can go to a trusted adult for help, they are more likely to discuss anything that may be important to them.

MATERIALS NEEDED

• list of situations (listed below)

• 2 large signs (one marked "tattling," or alternatively, the terms commonly used by the children, e.g., "squealing" or "ratting") and one marked "telling"

INSTRUCTIONS

1. This activity requires a large space (e.g., gym). Begin this activity by asking the class what "tattling" means to them. Then ask them to consider what "telling" means.

2. Discuss the differences between the two actions. *Ensure they understand that tattling is done to get someone in trouble while telling is done because someone is worried about a situation and wants to get help.*

3. Put up 2 big signs, "Tattling" and "Telling" on opposite walls of the gym.

4. Ask the children to:

   • listen to the situations, one at a time

   • decide whether it is tattling or telling

   • run to the wall and stand under the sign they believe describes the situation correctly.

   Situations:

   • You see your best friend picking on a younger child on the playground. (Telling)

   • Someone is emptying all the Lego pieces in the block corner. (Tattling)

   • You see an older boy stealing from the local corner store. (Telling)

   • You see an older boy stealing from the local corner store. He knows that you have been watching and threatens to hurt you if you tell someone. (Telling)

   • Your younger brother is throwing around his teddy bear. (Tattling)

   • Your aunt always pinches your cheek too hard when she comes to visit. (Telling)

   • Your friend reaches for a glass and accidentally knocks over a vase, spilling water all over the floor. (Tattling)

HOW & WHERE TO GET HELP CONT'D.

DISCUSSION QUESTIONS

- Was it hard to tell the difference between tattling and telling? Why? Why not?

- What usually happens when you tattle on someone?

- What usually happens when you tell someone about something to get help?

HOW & WHERE TO GET HELP CONT'D.

ACTIVITY: SEEKING HELP

When children seek help, they may give up if their first attempt is unsuccessful. This activity reinforces the concept of continuing to ask for help until someone is able or willing to help.

MATERIALS NEEDED

- matching pairs of cards, puzzle pieces or toys/objects

- small paper bags — 1 for each child

INSTRUCTIONS

1. Prepare matching pairs of cards, puzzle pieces or small toys/objects.

2. Place one item in each bag and fold the top.

3. Use an open space (e.g., gym, outdoors) to allow the children to move around freely.

4. Give each child one closed bag and tell them to look inside the bag at their object, without showing anyone else the object.

5. Explain to the children that this is a game where they have to find who has the object that matches theirs.

6. Ask the children to begin by choosing one person to ask *"What is in your bag?"* If the first person a child encounters does not have the matching object, s/he will move to a second person to ask and so on, until the children with each matching pair have found one another.

7. Tell the children to either sit down or form a circle when they have found their matching partner.

DISCUSSION QUESTIONS

- What did you do when the first person you asked didn't have the matching object?

- If you asked someone for help, but the person couldn't help you, what would you do?

Note to Facilitator: As a variation for older children, explain that the children may <u>not</u> name the object they are looking for, but rather may only use hints and clues as to what is in their bag (e.g., a child is looking for the matching piece of a horse puzzle might say *"It eats hay and you can ride it"*).